"Those who seek for glory in war
will not find it on the beaches of Dieppe.
Those who seek tales of valour
need look no further."

— **Robin Neillands, *The Dieppe Raid***

DIEPPE

Canada's Darkest Day of World War II

HUGH BREWSTER

SCHOLASTIC CANADA LTD.

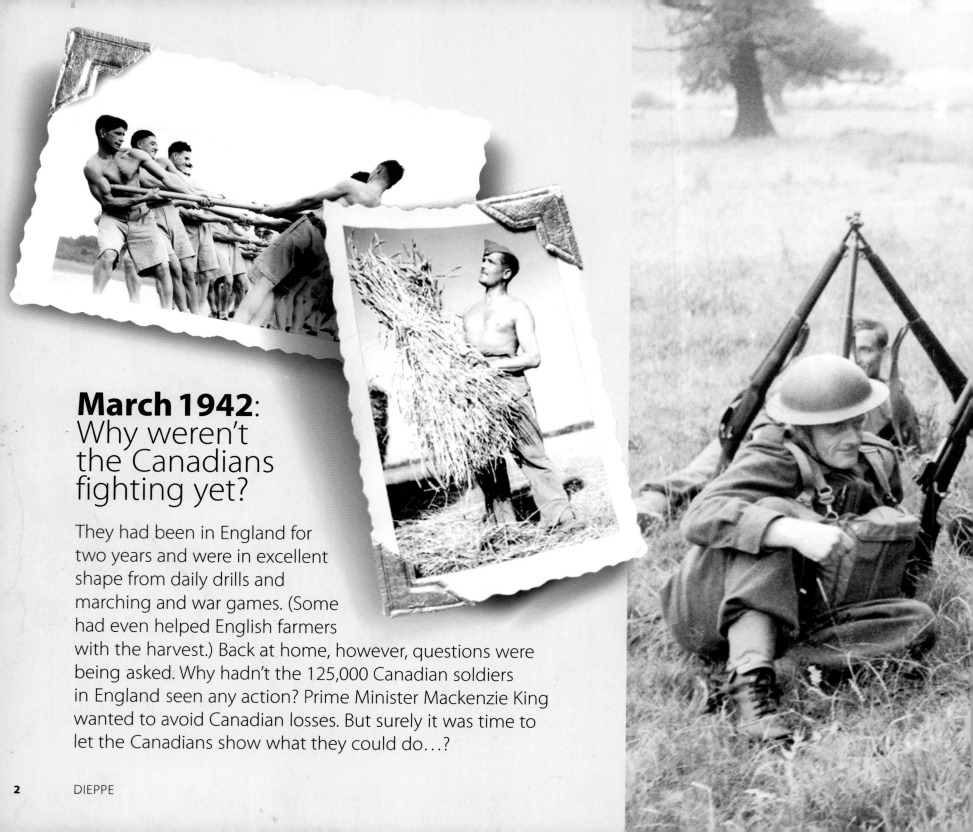

March 1942:
Why weren't the Canadians fighting yet?

They had been in England for two years and were in excellent shape from daily drills and marching and war games. (Some had even helped English farmers with the harvest.) Back at home, however, questions were being asked. Why hadn't the 125,000 Canadian soldiers in England seen any action? Prime Minister Mackenzie King wanted to avoid Canadian losses. But surely it was time to let the Canadians show what they could do…?

The **War** to Date

SEPTEMBER 3, 1939: Great Britain declares war on Germany after Hitler invades Poland; Canada declares war one week later

APRIL–MAY 1940: Nazis invade Denmark, Norway, Belgium, the Netherlands and France

MAY 10, 1940: Winston Churchill becomes Britain's prime minister

MAY 26–JUNE 4, 1940: Allied troops are rescued from Dunkirk on coast of France

JUNE 23, 1940: Hitler tours conquered Paris

SEPTEMBER–DECEMBER 1940: Heavy German bombing of Britain

APRIL 1941: Greece and Yugoslavia surrender to Hitler

JUNE 22, 1941: Germany invades the Soviet Union

DECEMBER 7, 1941: Japanese bomb U.S. base at Pearl Harbor; the U.S. and Britain then declare war on Hitler's ally, Imperial Japan

DECEMBER 11, 1941: Germany declares war on the United States

JANUARY 26, 1942: First U.S. troops arrive in Britain

ALLIED-CONTROLLED

AXIS-CONTROLLED

NEUTRAL

ICELAND

NORWAY

Vaagso

SWEDEN

FINLAND

SOVIET UNION

Leningrad (St. Petersburg)

Moscow

LATVIA

DENMARK

LITHUANIA

Furthest point of German advance

NORTHERN IRELAND

IRELAND

GREAT BRITAIN

LONDON

Newhaven

English Channel

Dunkirk

Dieppe

Berlin

GERMANY

POLAND

UKRAINE

CZECHOSLOVAKIA

St. Nazaire

PARIS

AUSTRIA

HUNGARY

ROMANIA

SWITZERLAND

FRANCE

YUGOSLAVIA

BULGARIA

SPAIN

ITALY

ROME

ALBANIA

TURKEY

PORTUGAL

GREECE

Spring 1942: **Hitler** is Winning

"I have [recently] had for the first time since the war started a growing conviction that we are going to lose. … It is all desperately depressing."

— **Chief British Commander Sir Alan Brooke, in his diary, March 31, 1942**

Winston Churchill (above) became prime minister of Great Britain on May 10, 1940, at the age of 65. (Right) Hitler tours Paris in June of 1940 after his forces had occupied the city. A year later, the Nazis invaded the Soviet Union and by 1942 Russian leader Joseph Stalin (below) was demanding help from Churchill.

The war was going badly for Britain and its allies. The United States had recently joined in the fight against Hitler and was sending troops and arms. But German submarines were sinking too many of the ships bringing supplies across the Atlantic.

Soviet Russia was another ally. With Hitler's tanks already inside Russia's borders, however, Soviet leader Joseph Stalin needed help. He wanted the British to mount an attack across the English Channel on German-occupied France. This would force Hitler to divert some of his forces from Russia to defend France. The United States agreed and President Roosevelt urged the British to attack — even if it would be a "sacrifice invasion" — to help relieve the Russians. Prime Minister Winston Churchill knew that an invasion of France in 1942 was a bad idea. "The waters of the Channel would be red with the blood of our lads," he stated.

But still his allies were insisting — even threatening. Britain must *do* something.

Rescue at **Dunkirk**

Two years before, when Hitler's armies had overrun France, thousands of British soldiers were trapped near the town of Dunkirk. Between May 26 and June 4, 1940, dozens of ships — along with small pleasure boats, fishing vessels and coastal ferries — raced across the Channel to bring back 338,000 soldiers. The "miracle of Dunkirk" gave such a boost to British morale that Winston Churchill had to remind his people that a rescue was not a victory. He knew that guns and tanks and tons of equipment had been left behind in France — leaving Britain in no shape to invade Hitler's Europe. But they had to show the world they were not defeated.

Making **Raids**

Right after Dunkirk a proposal landed on Winston Churchill's desk. It suggested the formation of a small, secret force of commandos. Their job would be to strike at the enemy, create havoc and then retreat. A select group of soldiers was immediately sent for intensive training in the Scottish Highlands. On the night of June 23, 1940, a raiding party of 120 men crept across the Channel, attacked some German positions on the French coast, and escaped with no casualties. The newspapers cheered. Soon, plans for even bigger, more ferocious raids were afoot.

(Left and top) British commandos training for enemy raids.

Harassing **Hitler**

Flames consume warehouses and factories (above) after a commando raid (below) on the port of Vaagso in German-occupied Norway on December 27, 1941. This raid forced Hitler to send forces to defend the Norwegian coast. Three months later, a British destroyer rammed into the gates of a giant dry dock in St. Nazaire, France. Loaded with delayed-action explosives, the ship soon blew up and wrecked the whole facility. This left the dreaded German battleship *Tirpitz* with no place to berth for repairs in France. But of the 611 men who raided St. Nazaire, only 242 returned.

Let the Canadians **Fight!**

"In a few months' time…
the Canadian army may find
itself engaged in one of the
bloodiest affrays that the
world has ever known…."

— Winston Churchill, in a speech to the
British House of Commons, December 1941

Canadian general Harry Crerar, at left, and British general Bernard "Monty" Montgomery.

The success of the commando raids on Hitler's Europe was not lost on the Canadian generals. They lobbied hard for Canadians to be used in a raid, claiming that their "inactivity" was bad for morale. They also lobbied Prime Minister Mackenzie King until he reluctantly gave his permission for Canadian soldiers to be used in "minor" raids.

The Russians and the Americans, meanwhile, continued to push for an invasion of France in 1942 — to be called Operation Sledgehammer. Winston Churchill wanted to avoid Sledgehammer at all costs. But when a large raid across the Channel was proposed, the prime minister supported it enthusiastically. The new "super-raid" would be code-named Operation Rutter.

On April 27, 1942, Canadian general Harry Crerar was summoned to British commander Bernard Montgomery's headquarters and told of the plan to raid an enemy-held port.

"Do you want it?" asked Montgomery briskly.

"You bet," Crerar replied.

"We were *not* spoiling for a fight!"

"The propaganda doled out to the Canadians back home — that we were bored and demoralized — is pure nonsense. ... Canadian troops were *not* spoiling for a fight. ... We certainly didn't feel we were 'languishing.' Our job was to defend England from enemy invasion."

— Captain Denis Whitaker, Royal Hamilton Light Infantry

Planning Operation Rutter

"There were far too many authorities with a hand in it...."
— General Montgomery (left) on the planning for the Dieppe Raid

Dieppe was one of several French ports targeted for possible raids early in 1942. Only 107 kilometres across the Channel, it was thought to be lightly defended and to have beaches suitable for landings. An important enemy radar station stood on the cliffs west of the town. Perhaps 500 commandos could knock it out? Soon, however, Dieppe was selected as a site for a larger raid — one that might satisfy the Russians and the Americans. And using Canada's 2nd Infantry Division would satisfy the clamour for action by the Canadian generals as well.

A team headed by Lord Louis Mountbatten quickly prepared an attack plan that would involve 5,000 men. But each time the plan was reviewed by the British Chiefs of Staff, changes were made. A flank attack from the sides of the town was changed to a frontal assault on the town itself. Heavy advance bombing of Dieppe was rejected for fear of civilian casualties. Mountbatten requested that a battleship provide covering fire for the attacking troops — but the navy thought the ship would be a sitting duck for enemy aircraft. "A battleship in the Channel in broad daylight?" one British admiral growled at Mountbatten. "You must be mad, Dickie!"

(Below) Lord Louis "Dickie" Mountbatten, a relative of the king, was young, handsome and ambitious. In 1941 he was appointed chief of Combined Operations, which was responsible for planning raids. (Opposite) Before the war, Dieppe was a popular seaside resort town with a large casino. (Right) A simulated strategy document shows how the plans for Operation Rutter were changed.

Operation Rutter:
Keys to Success

1. The enemy defences at Dieppe are weak.

2. The assault will take the enemy by surprise.

A frontal attack on the town

~~3.~~ It will be a "flank" assault — troops will land on either side of Dieppe and then move into the town.

~~4.~~ Heavy bomber aircraft will hit Dieppe before the attack, smashing gun posts, and demoralizing the enemy.

No Bombardment! air cover from fighter planes.

~~5.~~ Naval guns from large ships in the English Channel will provide covering gunfire for the troops landing on the beaches.

Covering fire from 6 small naval ships with 4-inch guns.

6. Paratroopers will land beforehand and attack and destroy the large guns on the coast that could fire on the landing ships.

7. Tanks will shepherd in the assault troops.

Training for the Raid

"The Canadians are first-class chaps; if anyone can bring it off, they will."

— General Montgomery

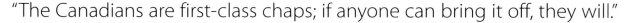

For four weeks, the troops of the Canadian 2nd Division trained hard — scaling cliffs, crawling through ditches and firing weapons. At dawn on June 12, 1942, they attempted a full-scale rehearsal of Operation Rutter. It was a shambles. Many soldiers landed on the wrong beaches, others were late and some got lost. The second run-through on June 23 went a little better — though, again, some of the troops landed behind schedule. "Fifteen minutes late," one British admiral noted, "could mean a disaster." But Mountbatten was satisfied enough to give Rutter the go-ahead.

On June 27, the raid's Canadian commander, Major-General Roberts, summoned his officers to a windowless room where he stood in front of a model of the Dieppe coastline. "Gentlemen," he stated, "we have waited more than two years to go into battle. . . . The time has now come." Most of the men were enthusiastic about the plan of attack, but when Roberts described it as "a piece of cake," one young officer whispered to Denis Whitaker, "a funny [expletive] piece of cake!"

On July 2, the men began boarding the troopships. Once everyone was on board, the commanders told the cheering soldiers that their destination would be Dieppe. For the next four days, the Canadians sweltered below decks in the July heat. The raid kept being postponed because the winds had to be just right for the paratroopers to be dropped inside France.

At dawn on July 7, four German planes spotted troopships lying at anchor off the Isle of Wight. They swooped down, strafing and bombing. Two ships were hit by bombs but, miraculously, only four men were slightly injured. By the next day the tides were no longer favourable and a message was sent from headquarters: "The operation against Dieppe has been cancelled."

(Below) Major-General John Hamilton 'Ham' Roberts, aged 50, was the Ground Force Commander for the Dieppe Raid. He supervised the training of the 2nd Division (opposite) and the rehearsals for Operation Rutter (above).

From Rutter to **Jubilee**

Two days after the cancellation, Canadian general Crerar received a letter from Army Command stating that the Dieppe Raid would be "off for all time." Within a week, however, Mountbatten had raised the idea with the Chiefs of Staff of remounting it. "All were startled," he later wrote, "and argued against it on security grounds." Mountbatten argued back that even if the enemy knew of the raid, they would never believe that the British would be stupid enough to attempt it again in the same place. He also said there was no time to find another target for a raid that year.

Winston Churchill was still under intense pressure from his U.S. and Russian allies to launch Operation Sledgehammer that summer. On July 22, he informed them that Sledgehammer had officially been abandoned. Stalin immediately sent a telegram demanding action to relieve his forces. Two days later, Churchill approved a remounting of the Dieppe Raid, to be named Operation Jubilee.

Ham Roberts said he was anxious to "get cracking as soon as possible." But not everyone was so confident. One of his officers wrote that when he heard about remounting the raid, "I knew at once that we were in for it."

Operation Jubilee: **The Plan**

Although the plans for Jubilee were similar to those for Rutter, some changes were made. The eight assaults along a 16-kilometre front were still to occur within one tide (six hours). But British commandos (with 50 U.S. Rangers) would replace paratroopers in taking out the big guns to the east and west of Dieppe.

(Below) The cliffs at Blue Beach.
(Right) A map used on the raid.

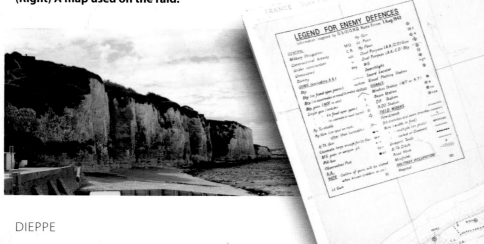

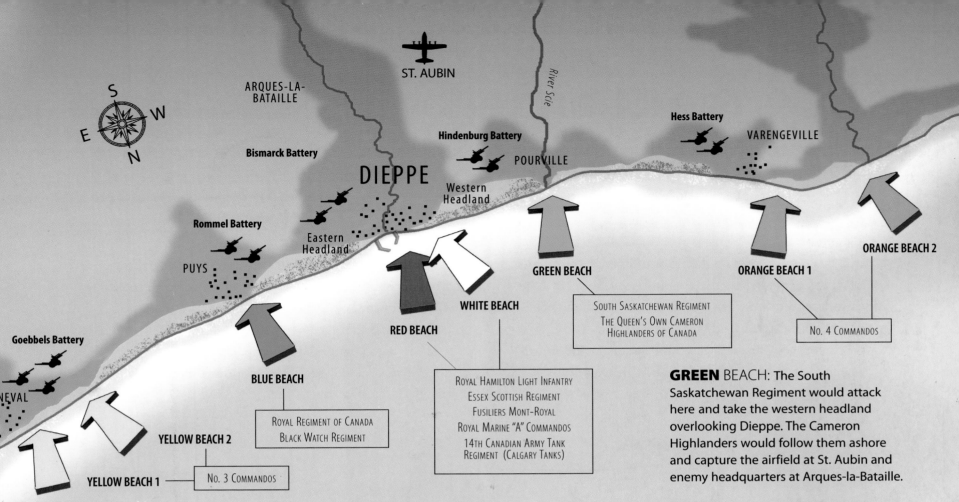

GREEN BEACH: The South Saskatchewan Regiment would attack here and take the western headland overlooking Dieppe. The Cameron Highlanders would follow them ashore and capture the airfield at St. Aubin and enemy headquarters at Arques-la-Bataille.

ORANGE BEACH 1 & 2: Two groups of No. 4 Commandos would destroy the Hess Battery 13.6 km west of Dieppe.

ROYAL **AIR FORCE**: Six squadrons of fighter planes would strike the headlands of Dieppe before the attack, while three squadrons would lay a smokescreen across the main beach as the landing craft approached the shore.

ROYAL **NAVY**: Four destroyers and a gunboat would bombard the front of the town before the landing craft arrived and then fire on the headlands.

RED BEACH: This eastern half of the long town beach was where the Essex Scottish Regiment would go ashore.

WHITE BEACH: The Royal Hamilton Light Infantry were to land in front of the town's large casino. Both battalions would be followed in by tanks of the Calgary Tanks unit and were to capture and hold the town and harbour. Demolition units would blow up docks, bridges and radar stations. The Royal Marines would then arrive to tow enemy invasion barges back to England. The Fusiliers Mont-Royal were to be held offshore as reinforcements.

YELLOW BEACH 1 & 2: Two groups of No. 3 Commandos would land 9.6 km east of Dieppe to destroy the big guns of the Goebbels Battery (each gun battery was code-named for a famous German).

BLUE BEACH: The Royal Regiment of Canada was to attack the beach at the village of Puys, destroy the small Rommel Battery, and then take the eastern headland overlooking Dieppe.

Across the **Channel** by Night

"They drove us to Portsmouth, right in to the shipyards where we boarded the troop carriers. A sailor said to me, 'You know where we're headed — to Dieppe, to Dieppe!'"

— Private Jack Poolton, Royal Regiment of Canada

From five ports along England's south coast a flotilla of 237 ships departed on the evening of August 18, 1942. Minesweepers led the way to clear a path through the mines laid by the enemy off the French coast. The Channel was calm but, as Jack Poolton recalled, "I don't think anybody slept. We tried to doze off but you were thinking about what it was going to be like … I thought, geez, all these men, some of them are going to make it … and some aren't coming back."

At 3:47 a.m. a gunboat accompanied by 23 small landing boats crossed through the minefield. On board

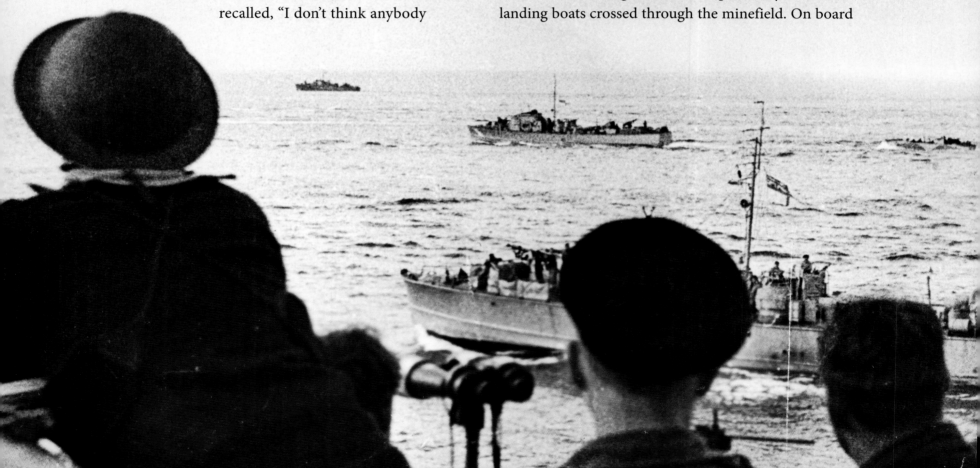

were the No. 3 Commandos headed for Yellow Beach. Suddenly, a flare lit up the sky. They had run into a German convoy heading into Dieppe harbour! A firefight erupted and after ten minutes the British gunboat was left badly damaged, with many of its crew wounded. The commandos' small landing boats had been scattered — and only six of them remained intact.

Major Peter Young knew there was no time to waste. His mission was to take out the big guns of the Goebbels Battery at Berneval, east of Dieppe. If left intact they could mow down the Canadians soon to attack the town. In his boat there were only 18 commandos. "My orders are to go ashore," he said to his men as they headed for the beach, "even if we have to swim."

(Above) Canadians board a transport ship and (left) take seats in a landing craft during a practice for the raid. (Below) The flotilla heads across the Channel towards Dieppe.

The **Commandos** Go In

YELLOW BEACH: 4:45 A.M. The sky was still dark as the boat with Peter Young's men scraped ashore on the pebbled beach. Ahead of them lay steep cliffs laced with barbed wire. Young spied a narrow gully in the chalk cliff and he and his men clawed their way up it. At the top of the cliff, they heard the big guns from the Goebbels Battery firing on the ships offshore. Clearly, the firefight with the convoy had alerted the enemy. After reaching the cornfields around the battery, Young's men opened fire, first with mortar bombs and then with their rifles and Tommy guns. Their sniping at the gun crews proved so infuriating that the Germans turned one of the huge guns around to fire at them. This delighted Major Young, since the gun couldn't fire low enough to hit them — and the shells whizzed over their heads. It also meant they weren't firing on the Canadians due to land on the beaches below.

After an hour and a half, Young decided to withdraw his men, as it was now full daylight. When they reached the cliffs, German soldiers began shooting at them as they clambered down towards their boat. Under heavy fire, they crawled into the boat with some of the men dragging it off the stones into the shallow water. By 10:45 that morning Young and all 18 of his men were back in England.

Major Peter Young (below, left) and his men scaled cliffs (right) similar to these. (Opposite, far left) Commandos give the "thumbs up" sign as they head back to England. (Opposite, centre) A landing craft returns to Newhaven, and (near left) the commandos come ashore feeling their mission has been a success.

Charging the **Hess Battery**

While Peter Young and his men were distracting the guns at Berneval, the men of the No. 4 Commandos were firing on the Hess Battery 20 km away, on the far side of Dieppe. In a lucky shot, they dropped a mortar bomb into a pile of ammunition, causing a huge explosion. Then, with bayonets drawn, 164 of the commandos swarmed over the battery "yelling like banshees." Captain Pat Porteous had a bullet pass through his hand and into his arm. Undeterred, he led an attack on a gun-pit where another bullet hit his leg. Staggering onwards, Porteous continued to lead his men as they fought their way across the battery. When all was quiet, they placed explosives in the huge gun barrels, splitting them open like bananas. Carrying away their wounded, the No. 4 Commandos withdrew to Orange Beach. From his boat in the Channel, their commander sent a message to Ham Roberts on the *Calpe*: "Hess Battery destroyed — is this okay with you?"

(Below) This gully is where the No. 4 Commandos climbed up after leaving their boats (opposite) at Orange Beach. They later broke through the barbed wire around the Hess Battery. Captain Pat Porteous (near left) won a Victoria Cross for his bravery during the charge on the battery.

Landing in **Hell**

"It would have been difficult to discover anywhere on the coast of Europe a less favourable area for an assault landing."

— **D.J. Goodspeed, historian of the Royal Regiment of Canada**

BLUE BEACH: 5:07 A.M. The Royal Regiment was late. Their attack plan for Blue Beach depended on surprise under cover of darkness, but they arrived just as dawn was breaking. Inside their machine-gun bunkers, the German defenders onshore were on full alert. They waited until the first nine landing craft hit the pebbled beach, watching as the ramps were kicked down and the Canadians sprinted ashore. Then they opened fire. Within minutes Blue Beach was carpeted with dead and wounded men. Those still on the landing craft had to climb over the bodies of men killed before them. Of the 250 men in the first wave, only a handful made it across the narrow beach to crouch below the seawall.

Then the second wave came ashore. To Jack Poolton, the bullets hitting his landing craft sounded like hail on a tin roof. He jumped into the water and staggered onto the beach

Enemy fire from the cliffs (top) rained down on the Canadians (above, left) at Blue Beach. Within hours, 225 young men lay dead by the seawall (above, right) and 264, including Jack Poolton (opposite, inset) were taken prisoner. (Opposite) The seawall at Blue Beach today.

while machine-gun fire kicked up the stones at his feet. "As the smoke cleared and I saw the carnage I knew I had landed in hell," he later wrote. Poolton hit the ground as a bullet hit the rim of his helmet. He could hear bullets thudding into the dead bodies around him.

Ten minutes later, at 5:45 a.m., a third wave of soldiers was sent in. Five landing craft with men from the Black Watch Regiment landed at the western end of the beach below steep cliffs. German gunfire from the top of the cliffs prevented them from providing any aid to their comrades pinned down on the beachfront. There, the hail of bullets and mortar bombs continued and, as the tide came in, wounded men were drowning. Amid all the smoke and noise, Jack Poolton heard a voice yell, "Sir, they're demanding that we surrender."

At 8:30 a.m. an undershirt was hoisted on a bayonet. For the men of the Royal Regiment still alive, the only choice left was death or captivity.

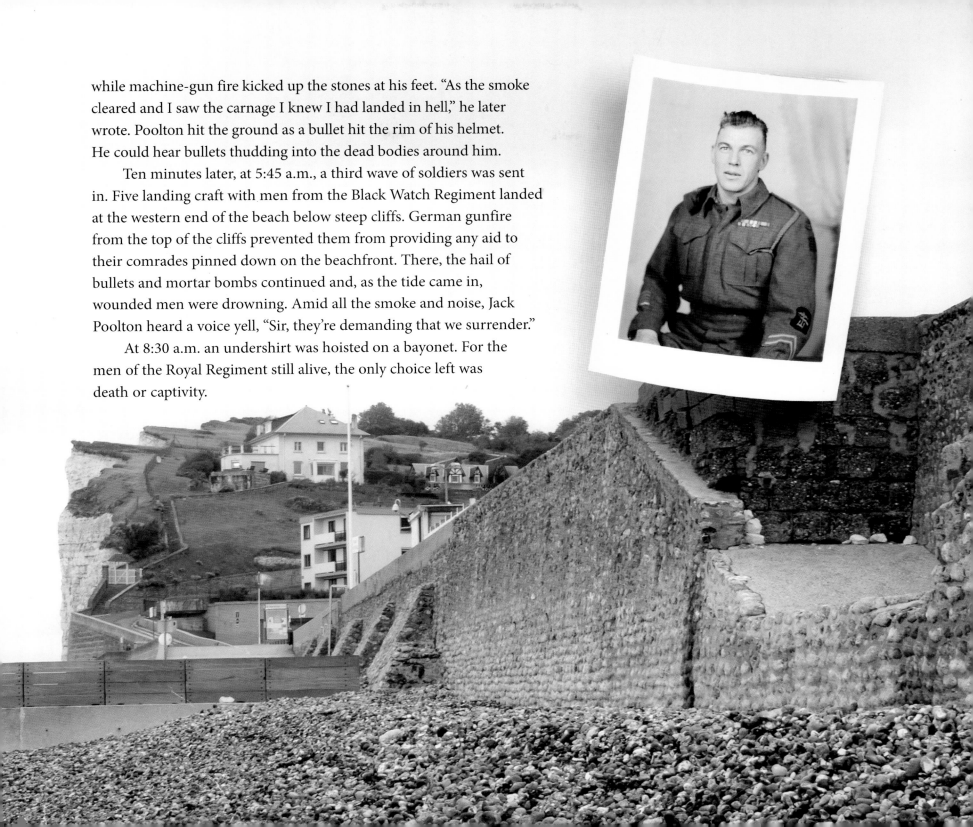

Attack at **Green** Beach

POURVILLE: 4:50 A.M. "As our small boats crept into the shore we could see lights shining in some windows and smoke curling from a few chimneys," recalled an officer of the South Saskatchewan Regiment. The fact that all was peaceful in the village of Pourville, just 4 kilometres to the west of Dieppe, was a good sign. Maybe here the enemy would be taken by surprise.

When their boots hit the beach pebbles it sounded "like a herd of elephants charging across a field of walnuts" to one of the prairie soldiers. But not a single shot was fired as they hacked their way through barbed wire towards the seawall. All was calm until the sound of the landing craft reversing off the beach caused enemy flares to light up the dawn sky. By then the South Saskatchewans were inside Pourville and their commanding officer, Lt-Colonel Charles Cecil Merritt, had set up temporary headquarters in a garage. His men quickly secured the town and the western cliffs, surprising some German officers who were in bed when their quarters were attacked.

Elation at their early success soon turned to dismay when

Green Beach: **The Plan**

The South Saskatchewan Regiment was to land three companies on the east side of the River Scie and one on the west side. B Company would land on the west side, move into Pourville and then clear the slopes to the west. C Company would land to the east of the river but then also advance to the western slopes. A and D Companies would clear the beach, capture the radar station on the eastern cliffs, attack an enemy headquarters at Quatre Vents Farm, and then clear the western headland above Dieppe. The Queen's Own Cameron Highlanders were to land behind the Saskatchewans and move inland along the eastern bank of the Scie to meet up with the tanks coming from the attack on Dieppe, and capture the airfield at St. Aubin. They would then destroy a major gun battery and attack the suspected German divisional headquarters at Arques-la-Bataille. What actually happened is shown at right.

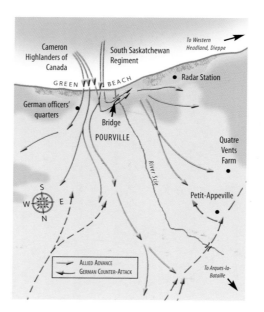

(Top) The beach at Pourville as it looks today. (Above, inset) Flyers were given out to French civilians telling them the attack was just a raid and not an invasion. (Opposite) Lt-Colonel "Cec" Merritt urges his men across the bridge.

the commanders realized that the battalion had landed in the wrong place — on the western side of the River Scie. Only one company should have landed there. The other three should have landed on the eastern side of the river. This meant that before A and D Companies could advance on the headland to the west of Dieppe they had to cross a narrow bridge over the river. And that bridge was already under heavy fire from enemy machine guns and mortars.

On hearing this, Lt-Colonel Merritt approached the bridge, twirling his helmet in his hand. He sauntered onto the bridge and called back, "Come on, boys, they can't hit a thing. Come on, let's go and get 'em." Through a hail of

gunfire, Merritt led a group of men across the bridge, some of them falling as they were hit. Merritt encouraged another group to cross, and then another. After bringing the last group over, Merritt was still unscathed, though many bodies lay by the roadside. He then decided to take out the pillbox gun emplacement that had been spitting fire at them. With only smoke as cover, he ran up the road and tossed a grenade right into the gun slit of the pillbox, and dived away as it exploded.

Despite these brave actions, Merritt's battalion soon found it could proceed no further. The enemy was now on full alert and manning the guns on the cliffs between them and Dieppe. To advance any further would be suicide.

The **Camerons** Come Ashore

GREEN BEACH: 5:50 A.M. The wail of the bagpipes was heard over the water as Corporal Alec Graham stood up in his landing craft and piped the Cameron Highlanders towards Green Beach. The pipes were soon drowned out, however, by the whoosh of enemy shells falling between the landing craft. Coolly calling out orders, the Camerons' commanding officer, Lt-Colonel Ryan Gostling, guided his men ashore. But only minutes after stepping onto the beach, Gostling was killed by machine-gun fire, and his second-in-command, Major Tony Law, quickly took charge.

Another blow for the Camerons was that, like the Saskatchewans, many of their boats had mistakenly landed on the west side of the River Scie.

In a quick change of plans, the Camerons on the east side of the river were told to join up with the Saskatchewans. Major Law then led the rest of his soldiers up the Scie valley, hoping to meet up with the Calgary Tanks that were supposed to be coming from Dieppe. The Germans, however, knew that the bridge at the village of Petit-Appeville was a key crossing and had sent a platoon of soldiers on bicycles and an anti-tank company to defend it. With that route blocked, Law decided to attack the German headquarters at Quatre Vents Farm but, on their way there, they came under overwhelming fire and decided to retreat to Pourville.

The Camerons who had joined up with the Saskatchewans, meanwhile, had advanced towards Quatre Vents Farm and the radar station on the cliffs but they, too, were halted by enemy fire and forced to retreat. Back on the beach, a message was received from the command ship *Calpe* to prepare for withdrawal at 11:00 a.m. But with the enemy closing in, an escape from Green Beach was looking more and more perilous.

This Man Must Not Be Taken **Alive!**

Jack Nissenthall, 24, (right) landed at Green Beach with ten Canadians who had orders to shoot him rather than let him be captured. Jack was a British radar expert whose top-secret mission was to get inside the German radar station on the cliffs above Pourville and steal key components. (Under torture, he might reveal the secrets of British radar — so he could not be taken alive.) Nissenthall and some of the Canadians managed to climb up to the radar station, but could not attack it because of intense enemy fire. Nissenthall was eventually able to crawl up its back wall and cut the power lines. He then knew he had to either escape or die. Back on Green Beach, Nissenthall and one Canadian dashed across the pebbles through a hail of bullets, swam out to a landing craft, and were back in England before nightfall. Meanwhile, the radar station where Nissenthall had cut the wires had switched to radio-telephone, and British tracking stations were able to monitor its signals. From this, the Allies learned much about German radar, including how to jam the enemy's radar system — a huge help during air raids later in the war.

(Opposite, left) The Camerons board the landing craft for the trip to Green Beach. (Opposite, right) Alec Graham plays the bagpipes as shells fall. This is the last time a Canadian regiment was piped into battle. (Inset) A badge of the Queen's Own Cameron Highlanders who were from Winnipeg. (Right) German soldiers climb the cliffs in pursuit of the attacking Canadians. (Far right) A radar station similar to the one at Pourville.

The **Assault** on Dieppe

WHITE BEACH: 5:23 A.M. The windows of the buildings on Dieppe's seafront glistened in the sun's first rays. "Why weren't they all damaged from the advance bombing?" thought Captain Denis Whitaker just as machine-gun bullets smashed against his landing craft. "My stomach jumped up to my throat," he later wrote. "This was it! The ramp dropped. I led the thirty-odd men of my platoon in a charge up the stony beach. We fanned out and flopped down just short of a huge wire obstacle. Bullets flew and mortar bombs crashed down . . . men were being hit and bodies were piling up everywhere."

Whitaker's Royal Hamilton regiment and the men of the Essex Scottish were meant to be covered by fire from the tanks of the Calgary Tanks regiment. But the tanks arrived late and some of them broke down as stones got stuck in their tracks. Pinned down with his men, Whitaker could see a stalled tank with its huge gun shattered by an enemy shell. Looking for a way to get his men off the beach before they were annihilated, he saw a white stucco building — the town's casino — off to his right. "Follow me! Make for the casino!" he yelled. They laid down smoke canisters as they ran. A pillbox right in front of the casino was silenced by a thrown grenade and they then cut their way through the barbed wire at the entrance. "The building was filled with Germans — two or three dozen — many of whom threw up their hands," Whitaker recalled. A room-by-room fight followed but at 7:00 a.m. General Roberts on the command ship *Calpe* received a message: CASINO TAKEN.

"It was a lot of murder coming down on us. Yes, of course I was scared. It was chaos! I slid under a tank that was not in action, and I thought, 'This was a good place, nobody was going to get me here, big Churchill tank on top of me.' However, the tank caught fire, and I very quickly got out from underneath there and I ran down the beach and there was a Tank Landing Craft beached in the water. It was listing, and we went around to the water side and that was another safe place. Nothing could touch you there! And then the tide began coming in. With the tide came the bodies."

— **Fred Engelbrecht, Royal Hamilton Light Infantry**

Tanks, Ships and Planes

"This is the first time that the British have had the courtesy to cross the sea to offer the enemy a complete sample of their weapons."

— Adolf Hitler

"You couldn't pick worse terrain for a tracked vehicle," recalled Major Allan Glenn of the Calgary Tanks. Although the beach stones did stall some of the brand-new Churchill tanks, 15 of the 29 tanks that were landed made it onto the promenade beyond the seawall. There, they soon discovered that all the streets into the town were blocked by concrete barriers. The Canadian Engineers,

known as "sappers," were supposed to blow up these obstacles, but they were mostly lying dead on the beach. (Of the 169 sappers who went ashore, 152 were killed, wounded or captured.) This meant that the tanks could only rumble around the promenade firing their guns until their ammunition ran out. Some of them returned to the beach to try and help there.

Damaged Churchill tanks (below) sit on the Dieppe beachfront after the raid. (Opposite, top) Guns from a destroyer fire on Dieppe. (Opposite, bottom) HMS _Berkeley_ was hit by a German bomber. Its crew was rescued before it was sunk by a British torpedo.

The guns on the tanks could not reach the German gun batteries firing mercilessly from the headlands. When the four naval destroyers ventured close to the shore, their 4-inch guns were no match for the overwhelming German firepower either. To Raymond Geoffrion, pinned down on the beach, the firing was like "a big thunderstorm, tracer bullets coming from everywhere. We were all stuck there — praying and calling out for our mothers."

The Greatest **Air** Battle

At dawn, dozens of British Spitfires swept in over the chalk cliffs of Dieppe. They were so close to the ground the pilots could see the faces of the Nazi anti-aircraft gunners. Smoke bombs were dropped to provide cover for the troops about to land. Soon, more than 260 enemy Focke-Wulf and Messerschmitt fighters screamed in to attack the Allied flyers, and many smoking, spinning planes began crashing into the sea. When German Dornier bombers lumbered in to bomb the landing craft, they were swarmed by Spitfires. Canadian pilot "Duke" Warren remembers firing on one bomber and seeing flames erupt from its port engine. "The Dornier continued to dive but very soon the crew bailed out and it crashed near Dieppe Harbour." One thousand planes fought over Dieppe in the greatest one-day air battle of the war. It was also the greatest one-day loss for the British: 106 planes were downed and 67 crewmen (including 11 Canadians) were lost; 48 German planes were destroyed and 24 damaged.

(Above) Identical twins Bruce, left, and Douglas "Duke" Warren, 20, each flew a Spitfire (top) at Dieppe and shot down a Dornier bomber (above, right). Insignia of the German Luftwaffe (air force) decorate this Nazi armband (right).

Sending in the **Reserves**

THE COMMAND SHIP, **HMS CALPE**: 7:00 A.M. Ham Roberts had no idea just how badly the attack was going. A garbled radio message to the *Calpe* had told him that soldiers of the Essex Scottish Regiment were in the town. (A few men had indeed made it into the streets but most were either dead or pinned down on the beach.) This news encouraged Roberts to make his biggest mistake of the morning — sending in the reserves.

At 7:00 a.m., the men of the Fusiliers Mont-Royal prepared to go ashore in 26 small wooden boats. Their commander, Lt-Colonel Dollard Ménard, called out to his cheering men through a megaphone, "We'll show 'em what we're made of! Good luck, boys!" At full speed, the small flotilla charged towards the smokescreen shrouding the beach. As they passed through into the sunshine, they were greeted by an overwhelming roar of gunfire. Bullets tore into the sides of their boats, sinking two of them and scattering the others. Some boats landed, but, as Corporal Robert Berubé recalled, only 7 of the 20 men in his boat got across to the seawall. "The rest were all killed. We just stayed on the beach. You moved and you'd had it." His commander, Dollard Ménard, was hit by a bullet as he

(Above, right) Landing craft prepare to go onto the Dieppe beachfront and (below) approach the smokescreen that had been laid across the shore by destroyers (above, left).

landed, but continued to charge at a pillbox and was wounded four more times before passing out.

No news of this was reaching the *Calpe*, so at 8:00 a.m. Ham Roberts decided to send in his last reserves, the commandos of the Royal Marines. When their boats passed through the smokescreen, the commanding officer caught sight of the carnage onshore. He quickly waved to the boats behind him to go back — saving the lives of 200 men before he was shot and fell dead to the deck of his boat.

(Above) For the soldiers of the Fusiliers Mont-Royal who made it ashore, the beach was a scene of horror. (Right) A poster describes Dollard Ménard's bravery.

Ce qu'il faut
POUR VAINCRE

LE LIEUTENANT-COLONEL DOLLARD MÉNARD, D.S.O.,
COMMANDANT DES FUSILIERS DU MONT-ROYAL À DIEPPE.

En dépit de cinq blessures en cinq heures, le colonel Ménard poussa l'attaque à fond. A la fin, immobilisé par ses blessures, il persista quand même à organiser la défense antiaérienne et à veiller au rembarquement de ses hommes.

Vanquish Means **Withdraw!**

HMS *CALPE*: 9:00 A.M. IN SEVERE DIFFICULTY, MUST BE TAKEN OFF OR WILL BE WIPED OUT. This desperate message from the Fusiliers Mont-Royal finally managed to get through to the *Calpe* at 9:00 a.m. Even then, Ham Roberts was reluctant to admit failure. Finally, at 9:40, he realized that the assaults on Blue and Green Beaches had stalled and that the headlands above Dieppe could not be taken. With an ashen face he said softly, "Bring them home," and the coded withdrawal signal VANQUISH 1100 HOURS was sent out.

But "bringing them home" would be no easy task. On Green Beach, just after 11:00, four boats managed to approach the beach even though "the water around them was boiling from the number of mortar shells being exploded." When the men saw the boats, they stampeded. Through ferocious machine-gun fire they rushed towards the boats, some of them crawling, some dragging wounded friends. One of the boats became so overloaded that it sank; another was destroyed by shellfire.

(Top left) A radio message was finally sent from this scout car to Ham Roberts (below) on the *Calpe*, telling him of the disaster on the beach. (Above) Men who had swum out to sea are pulled onto a destroyer and (opposite) a wounded Canadian is taken ashore in England.

From the seawall, Lt-Colonel Merritt and some of his men fired back at the enemy to keep them at bay. When Merritt saw a wounded man lying in the water, he ran out to drag him under cover and was hit in the shoulder by a sniper's bullet — his only wound of the day.

On the main Dieppe beachfront, things were little better. Here, too, some of the boats that made it ashore quickly became overloaded, and capsized. Some men chose just to swim for it. By 12:20, the firing was so intense that the beaches could no longer be reached. The command ship *Calpe* made a last rescue attempt at 12:48 but was forced to retreat back into the smokescreen. A bitterly disappointed Ham Roberts instructed the fleet to sail for England. Some 3,367 men, 2,752 of them Canadians, remained on the beaches, dead or soon to be taken prisoner.

MEN of VALOR
They fight for you

"When last seen he was collecting Bren and Tommy Guns and preparing a defensive position which successfully covered the withdrawal from the beach." — Excerpt from citation awarding Victoria Cross to Lt.-Col. Merritt, South Saskatchewan Regt., Dieppe, Aug. 19, 1942

Lt-Colonel Merritt's actions during the withdrawal are celebrated in this poster. He would go into captivity with more than 250 men from Green Beach. Of the 1,026 Canadians who landed at Pourville, 685 would be killed, wounded or captured.

Surrender!

As the boats retreated, the firing on the beaches died down. On the main Dieppe beach, Fred Engelbrecht was lying in the water when suddenly "as far as I could see on the seawall were German soldiers. Then I heard, *'Hände hoch'* [hands up] and *'Kommen sie hier'* [come here]. I didn't speak German but I knew what they were saying."

On Blue Beach, where the fighting had ended earlier, Jack Poolton was horrified to see German officers "shooting the worst of the wounded, putting them out of their misery." But many more Canadians saw the humane side of their captors. One remembered a German soldier spooning soup into the mouth of a badly wounded Canadian in a house above Blue Beach. On Green Beach, a German soldier saw three Canadians clinging to an overturned landing craft offshore and swam out to rescue them, dodging fire from a British Spitfire overhead.

"My place is **with my boys**"

"Every man carry a man!" called out Chaplain John Foote of the Royal Hamilton Light Infantry as he lifted a wounded man and waded out to a landing craft. For more than an hour on the shell-torn Dieppe beachfront, the chaplain calmly carried over 30 men out to the boats. As the last boat was leaving, Foote was pulled on board, but he jumped into the water, saying, "My place is with my boys," and returned to the beach. A prisoner until May 1945, Foote is the only Canadian chaplain ever to be awarded the Victoria Cross.

Soon, from all the beaches, lines of captured soldiers with raised hands were marched into Dieppe. One Canadian took a last look at Red Beach and saw "a shambles of devastation … guts and limbs strewn about, bodies floating in the water and lapped by waves." For years, he and others who had survived would recall this scene of horror and ask, "For what?"

(Opposite, top) As Canadians raise their hands in surrender, two soldiers assist a friend who has been blinded. (Above) A German soldier gives first aid to a wounded Canadian. (Right) Newspapers first reported the raid as a great victory.

The Grim **Tally**

Of the 6,090 men who took part in the Dieppe landings, 4,384 were killed, wounded or missing — a loss of almost three-quarters of them. Of the 1,027 who were killed, 907 were Canadians. All the equipment landed on shore was lost. The Royal Navy had lost 550 men and 34 boats.

The March into **Captivity**

At the Dieppe hospital, the wounded lay in rows on the lawn. The nuns and doctors tried to give aid but they were overwhelmed. Early that evening a hospital train left for the city of Rouen carrying over 500 German and Allied wounded. All the captured soldiers who could walk were formed into long columns and marched out of Dieppe towards the town of Envermeu, 14 kilometres inland. Many of the men who had tried to swim away were missing pants, shoes or socks.

"I whispered, 'thank you, thank you' as they marched past," remembered civilian Georges Guibon. Other Dieppe citizens flashed the "V for victory" sign and tried to pass food or water to the Canadians. When the guards prevented this, one old woman pelted the captives with tomatoes while pretending to curse them. The soldiers gratefully ate the tomatoes.

"I am going to **take care** of you"

A young French nun, Sister Agnès Marie Valois (right), is remembered for her kindness to wounded Canadians in the Rouen hospital. One soldier who had lost his sight remembers her whispering to him, "Everything will be all right. I am a French nurse and I am going to take care of you, *mon petit soldat* [my little soldier]." In 1998, Sister Agnès was awarded Canada's Meritorious Service Medal.

(Opposite) Canadian prisoners are marched out of Dieppe. (Top, left) The hospital in Dieppe was overwhelmed with casualties. (Right) Newlyweds M and Mme Jean Dupuis leave the church at Envermeu (above). Mme Dupuis kept a coin the soldiers tossed to her.

On entering Envermeu, the soldiers passed a wedding party that had just left the parish church. The Canadians cheered the bride and groom and tossed coins to them. The best man noticed that a barefoot Canadian, Stan Darch of Hamilton, was limping badly. The man took off his new shoes and gave them to Darch.

(This gesture later caused his arrest.) That night the officers were billeted in the church, still filled with wedding flowers. The rest of the soldiers were herded into an unfinished factory with a dirt floor. Jack Poolton remembers that, nearly dying of thirst, he scraped a hole in the floor and pressed his parched lips and tongue into the damp earth.

The next morning at 6:00 a.m. the men were given a piece of black bread and the march to prison camp resumed.

Prisoners of War

The British prisoners in Stalag VIIIB cheered and waved as the Canadians from Dieppe marched into the camp. This welcome raised their spirits after five miserable days and nights spent in filthy railroad boxcars being transported across France and Germany. The British prisoners shared their daily ration of cabbage soup with the Canadians. Jack Poolton drank his out of his boot, as he had no bowl or spoon. The soup had sand and worms in it, but it was hot and Jack hadn't eaten in days. That evening some musical instruments were found in the camp and two fiddlers from Manitoba, along with a banjo player, performed country tunes.

But this was only a brief respite from the misery of camp life. Five weeks later, the Dieppe Canadians were marched before a German officer who ordered that their wrists be tied with ropes. A copy of the plan for the Dieppe raid had been found on the beach and in it were orders that any Germans taken prisoner should have their hands tied. Now, the same would be done to the Canadians until Winston Churchill apologized. "For two weeks our hands were tied in front of us, then for two weeks tied behind us," remembers Ron Reynolds of the Royal Regiment. The ropes caused ugly sores and were later replaced with shackles. The men soon found a way to unlock the shackles using the keys from the cans of corned beef that came in parcels from the Red Cross. But any prisoner found without his shackles was severely punished. "We were in shackles for one year, 44 days and 45 minutes," recalled Colonel Labatt of the Royal Hamilton Light Infantry.

The Canadians were left unshackled on Christmas Day, 1942, but it was still a lonely, hard day for men far away from food, carols and their loved ones.

Sweet is the name of Liberty, but the thing itself has a value beyond all inestimable Treasure

"Well, it was grim, just grim. There were bed bugs, fleas, lice, and rats. The place was just infested with bed bugs. And the fleas would get right inside your clothes. You slept with everything but your boots on because it was too cold otherwise — you only had one blanket."

— **Jack Poolton**

(Opposite, top) A longing for freedom is depicted in this painting of Stalag VIIIB. It is from one of the logbooks that were donated by the YMCA to Canadian prisoners. The barracks are shown in a photograph from a logbook (top) and in the artwork at centre and lower right. (Right) Prisoners depended on the food rations sent to them in these boxes by the Red Cross. (Opposite, bottom) A prisoner shows the shackles (centre) that the Canadians were made to wear for over a year.

Tunnels and Escapes

"We're going to dig a tunnel. Keep a tight lip." In early March of 1943, this message was passed from hut to hut in the Canadian compound. Even in shackles the Dieppe men were not going to give up. Beneath a bunk in the hut closest to the wire fence, a square was cut in the concrete floor and a shaft dug to a depth of 3 metres. The tunnel then had to go 43 metres out to come up in some trees beyond the fence. Secretly getting rid of the sandy soil from the tunnel required everyone's help. Fred Engelbrecht remembers filling his Red Cross box with sand and letting it leak out as he walked about the camp.

Jack Poolton helped make the digging tools. Supports for the tunnel were made with slats from the bunks. A trolley with tin-can wheels was built for the diggers, and air was pumped down to them from a bellows made from a kit bag. The escape committee was busy creating civilian clothing from blankets and dyed uniforms. Documents the escaping men would need were cleverly forged with official-looking stamps that were carved from a shoe heel or even a potato. By May the tunnel was ready to go. Over the next six months, 36 men crawled through it, two at a time. About half of them made it back to England — a record for any prison camp. When the tunnel was discovered, the men were threatened and punished, but soon they began digging another one.

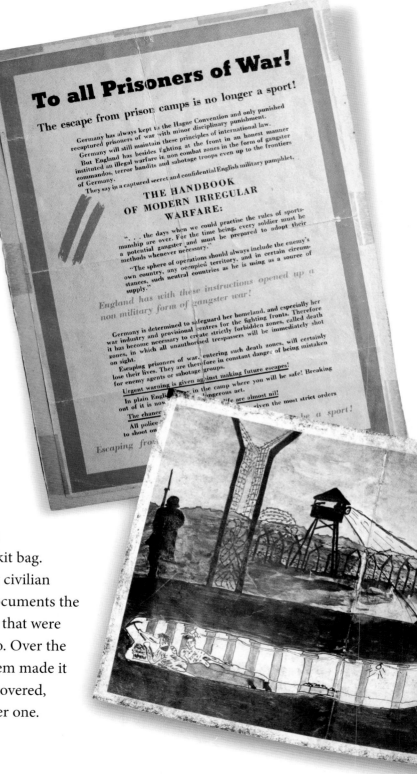

(Above) A prisoner descends into a tunnel to begin work while another (right) digs inside the shaft. (Left) A drawing from a prisoner's album shows air being pumped down into a tunnel as two men dig below. (Opposite, top) A German poster warns prisoners that "escaping is not a sport." (Opposite, left) Bedding and belongings are thrown out in the snow as camp guards search for a tunnel.

On their hidden radio the prisoners were jubilant to hear of the Allied landings in Normandy on D-Day, June 6, 1944. Soon they could see American planes flying overhead, making bombing raids on German towns. When Russian troops crossed into Germany in January 1945, the prisoners began to believe the war might be over soon. But for them, an even harsher ordeal was about to begin.

Death March and
Liberation

"I am on my way home. Every step is a step in the right direction. Don't give up now." Jack Poolton kept repeating these words to himself as he trudged through the snow and howling winds. He knew that if he fell behind he would be shot by the guards. The frozen bodies of other men lay by the roadside.

As the invading Russians had drawn near in late January of 1945, the Germans had marched their prisoners of war out of the camps at gunpoint. Through one of the coldest winters on record, a straggling column of men with frozen beards and eyebrows moved westward. At night they would sleep in barns or abandoned factories. Every few days they might be given a little black bread to eat. They scrounged what other food they could from farms and fields. Ron Reynolds remembers how he and some others dived into a pile of turnips and ate them raw, so desperate was their hunger.

On April 12, 1945, Jack Poolton was one of an exhausted group of prisoners sleeping in a barn near a town called Ditfurt. He had heard a rumour that advancing Allied troops were not far away. At 6:00 a.m. he was awakened by a voice shouting, "There's a jeep out there!" Jack ran outside and saw a jeep with three American soldiers in it. "I saw three angels that morning. We were liberated. I will never forget that day." Jack grabbed the rifle from one of the German guards at the barn door. The guard surrendered, saying, "I am the prisoner now."

The Americans were shocked at the emaciated state of the Canadian prisoners. Before long, they were sent to hospitals in England to recuperate. They would have loved to have been with their battalions in the Canadian 2nd Division on September 1, 1944, when Dieppe was liberated. "Instead of bullets and blood," one newsman reported, "Dieppe gave the Canadians flowers and wine. A delirious population poured into the streets to shout that the town was free."

(Opposite, top) Emaciated survivors of the death march. (Opposite, centre) Jack Poolton carried this homemade compass with him on the death march. (Opposite, bottom) Ron Reynolds is greeted by his family on his return to Canada. (Above, left) German soldiers are marched off under guard by the Americans in April 1945. (Centre) Defeated Germans leave Dieppe as prisoners before the Canadian 2nd Division are greeted as liberators (right) on September 1, 1944. Later that day, men of the Royal Hamilton Light Infantry (below) laid a wreath at the graves of men who died at Dieppe on August 19, 1942.

It **Haunts** Us Still

"On the beaches of Dieppe, our Canadian cousins marked with their blood the road to our final liberation."

— from the monument in Place du Canada, Dieppe

The people of Dieppe have never forgotten the Canadians and their sacrifice. Every August 19, Dieppe's streets are festooned with Canadian flags, and memorial services are held on the beaches and at the Canadian War Cemetery. The 65th anniversary commemoration in 2007 was especially memorable — many of the veterans attending knew it would be their last visit. When the band played "O Canada" and the old men saluted their lost comrades, there were very few dry eyes.

Why do the Dieppe veterans come back to this place of "bullets and blood"?

For some it helps to heal, if not to fully accept why 907 Canadians had to die there. Bitterness and anger remain to this day over what some historians call "the suicide raid." Jack Poolton always believed that "those who planned this disaster had to be idiots." An easy scapegoat was quickly found in the Canadian commander, Ham Roberts. Until his death in 1962, Roberts would receive a package in the mail each August 19. In it would be a small, stale piece of cake. Lord Louis Mountbatten, who was more deserving of blame, always vigorously defended the raid. "For every man who died at Dieppe in 1942," he maintained, "at least ten or more must have been spared in the invasion of Normandy in 1944." For years, this became

the official line on Dieppe — the "valuable lessons" it provided helped lead to victory. Certainly, the mistakes of Dieppe would not be repeated. But many believe that the price of learning was far too high.

Nevertheless, the soldiers who landed at Dieppe were among the 1.1 million Canadian men and women during World War II who enlisted to stop the most murderous tyrant the world had ever seen. We owe them so very much.

(Opposite, left) Veterans salute at the 65th-anniversary ceremony held near the cliffs of Blue Beach, below. (Opposite, right) Fred Engelbrecht rides a jeep in a parade along the Dieppe promenade on August 19, 2007. (Above, left) The grave of an 18-year-old soldier of the Fusiliers Mont-Royal. (Centre) Ron Reynolds pays his respects in the Canadian War Cemetery while Sister Agnès (right) reunites with Corporal Donatien Vaillancourt.

Dieppe **Veterans**

Two Canadians who had served at Dieppe, **Charles Cecil Merritt** and **John Foote**, were awarded the Victoria Cross, the highest award for gallantry in the British Commonwealth. **"Cec" Merritt** became a federal Member of Parliament for Vancouver-Burnaby in 1945 and served until 1949. He then practised law in Vancouver and died there in 2000 at the age of 91. The bridge over the River Scie in Pourville is today known as the Lieutenant-Colonel Merritt Bridge. **John Foote** also entered politics and served as an MP in the Ontario Legislature and eventually became a cabinet minister. He died in Cobourg, Ontario, in 1988. The James Street Armoury in Hamilton, Ontario, is named for him. **Dollard Ménard**, the only commanding officer at Dieppe to return alive to England, was awarded the Distinguished Service Order for his bravery. He became a brigadier-general in the Canadian army and was made a Grand Officer of the National Order of Quebec before his death in 1997. **Denis Whitaker** also won a DSO as the only officer who fought his way into town and escaped unwounded. He became a successful businessman and sportsman, heading Canada's Olympic Committee in 1980. He also wrote several books about military history before his death in 2001. **Jack Nissenthall** was never decorated for his achievement even though Lord Mountbatten claimed it helped shorten the war by two years. He returned to Pourville in 1967 for the 25th anniversary and there met **Les Thrussel**, the Canadian who had dashed to safety with him across Green Beach. At his funeral in 1997 in Toronto, where he had lived since 1978, Jack Nissenthall was hailed as the "unknown hero" of Dieppe.

It would take 52 years for a decoration recognizing Dieppe veterans to be created. The Dieppe bar (above) for the Volunteer Service Medal was finally awarded to veterans of the raid in 1994. Pension and health benefits were also slow in coming to the men who had suffered so much in prison camp and on the death march. **Jack Poolton** had nightmares for many years after his return home. In 1998 he published his story, *Destined to Survive*, and regularly gave talks in schools until his death in 2005. **Fred Engelbrecht** served for 35 years with the Hamilton Fire Department. He has returned to Dieppe three times since 1942, and hopes to go to the 70th anniversary in 2012. **Ron Reynolds** has returned frequently to Dieppe and wants to have his ashes scattered on Blue Beach. He lives today in Port Hope, Ontario. **Douglas "Duke" Warren** still misses his twin brother, Bruce, who died in 1961 during the test flight of a CF-100 jet fighter. Duke served with the RCAF for 37 years and retired in Comox, B.C. In 2007, he was awarded the French Legion of Honour for his actions in the skies over Dieppe.

Glossary

Allies: the nations — including Great Britain, the United States, the Soviet Union, Canada and others — that fought against Germany, Japan and Italy during World War II.

army units: The **Canadian army** during World War II had 5 **divisions**. The **2nd Infantry Division**, which fought at Dieppe, was made up of 3 **brigades**; each **brigade** had 3 **regiments** made up of 2 **battalions**. A **battalion** had 5 **companies** made up of 3 **platoons** of approximately 35 soldiers each.

artillery: weapons such as big guns and cannons.

battery: a defensive position from which guns are fired.

civilian: someone who is not an active member of the military or police.

commandos: members of a special fighting force used to make destructive raids. The name was first used in the Boer War.

convoy: a group of ships travelling together with a protective escort.

destroyer: a small, fast warship usually armed with guns and torpedoes.

dry dock: a large dock in the form of a basin from which the water can be emptied, used for building or repairing a ship below its water line.

flotilla: a fleet of small ships.

headland: a point of land, usually on water. The white chalk cliffs of Dieppe form headlands on either side of the town.

mine: a device containing explosives in a watertight casing, floating on or moored beneath the surface of the water for the purpose of blowing up an enemy ship.

minesweeper: a ship that clears away mines.

mortar: A portable cannon used to fire shells at high angles over short distances.

Nazi: a member of the political party headed by Adolf Hitler that held power in Germany from 1933–1945.

paratroopers: soldiers equipped and trained to parachute out of planes.

pillbox: a low-roofed concrete gun emplacement for a machine gun or anti-tank gun.

radar: a method of detecting distant objects by causing radio waves to be reflected from them, and analyzing the reflected waves.

sapper: a military engineer who lays or disarms mines or who constructs trenches or tunnels that undermine enemy positions. From the French verb *saper*, to undermine.

scout car: a small, fast military vehicle with four-wheel drive and an open top.

seawall: a wall built to protect a beach from being washed away.

shells/shellfire: explosive rounds fired by **artillery.**

Soviet Union: a former communist country that existed between 1922 and 1991 and included Russia and 14 other Soviet socialist republics.

squadron: a basic, tactical air force unit, or group of planes. Also a naval unit consisting of two or more **divisions** of a fleet.

strafe: to attack with a machine gun from a low-flying airplane. From the German verb *strafen*, to punish.

Tommy gun: a nickname for a Thompson submachine gun (seen in photo of Canadian soldiers on pages 8–9).

Index

Page numbers in italics refer to illustrations or maps.

A
Arques-la-Bataille, France, 15, 22

B
Berkeley, HMS, 28, *29*
Berneval, France, 15, 17
Berubé, Corporal Robert, 30
Black Watch Regiment of Canada, 15, 21
Blue Beach, 14, 15, 20–21, *20–21*, 32, 34, *44–45*, 46
Brooke, Sir Alan, 5

C
Calgary Tanks (14th Canadian Army Tank Regiment), 15, 25, 26
Calpe, command ship, 19, 25, 26, 30–31, 32
Cameron Highlanders (Queen's Own) of Canada, 15, 22, 24–25, *24*
Canadian 2nd (Infantry) Division, 42–43, 46
Canadian Engineers (Royal), 28

Churchill, Prime Minister Winston, 4, 5, *5*, 6, 7, 8, 9, 14, 38
commandos, 7, 18–19, 46
Crerar, General Harry, 9, *9*, 14

D
Darch, Stan, 37
Dieppe, France,
air battle, 29
assault on Dieppe, 26–27
before war, 10
convoy headed for Dieppe, 17
Dieppe 65th anniversary, 44–45
plan for raid, 14–15
planning Dieppe Raid, 10–11
prisoners leaving Dieppe, 36–37
sending in reserves, 30–31
surrender, 34–35
tanks on Dieppe beach, 28–29
training for raid, 12–13
withdrawal, 32–33
Dunkirk, France, 4, 6, 7
Dupuis, M and Mme Jean, *37*, *37*

E
Engelbrecht, Private Fred, 26, *26*, 34, 40, *44*, 46
Envermeu, France, 36–37
Essex Scottish Regiment, 15, 26, 30

F
Foote, Chaplain John (Captain), 34, *34*, 46
(Les) Fusiliers Mont-Royal (FMR), 15, 30–31, 45

G
Geoffrion, Raymond, 29
Glenn, Major Allan, 28
Goebbels Battery, 15, 17, 18
Gostling, Lt-Col. Ryan, 24
Green Beach, 15, *22*, 22–23, 24–25, 32–33, 34, 46
Guibon, Georges, 37

H-I-J
Hamilton *Spectator*, 35, *35*
Hess Battery, 15, 19
Hindenburg Battery, 15
Hitler, Adolf, 4, 5, *5*, 6, 7, 9, 28, 45
Isle of Wight, 13
Jubilee, Operation, 14–15

K-L-M
King, Prime Minister Mackenzie, 2, 9
Labatt, Lt-Col. Robert, 38
Law, Major Tony, 24–25
Ménard, Lt-Col. Dollard, 30–31, *31*, 46
Merritt, Lt-Col. Charles Cecil, 22–23, 32–33, *33*, 46
Montgomery, Lt-Gen. Bernard, 9, *9*, 10, *10*, 12
Mountbatten, Lord Louis, 10, 11, *11*, 12, 14, 44, 46

N-O-P-Q
Newhaven, England, 4, 19
Nissenthall, Jack, 25, 46
No. 3 Commandos (British), 15, 17, 18–19
No. 4 Commandos (British), 15, 18–19
Orange Beach, 15, 19
Poolton, Private Jack, 16, 20–21, *21*, 34, 37, 38, 39, 40, 41, 42, 43, 44, 46
Porteous, Captain Pat, 19, *19*
Pourville, France, 15, 22–23, 24–25, 26, 33
Quatre Vents Farm, 24–25

R
Red Beach, 15, 35
Reynolds, Ron, 38, 42, *42*, 45, *45*, 46
Roberts, Maj-Gen. Hamilton, 13, *13*, 14, 19, 26, 30–31, 32, *32*, 44
Rommel Battery, 15
Roosevelt, President Franklin, 5
Rouen, France, 36–37
Royal Air Force, 15
Royal Hamilton Light Infantry Regiment (RHLI), 9, 15, 26, 38, 43, 46
Royal Marines, 15, 31
Royal Navy, 15, 35
Rutter, Operation, 10–11, 12–13, 14

S-T
Scie, River, 15, 22–23, 24–25, 46
Sledgehammer, Operation, 9, 14
South Saskatchewan Regiment, 15, 22–23, 24–25
St. Aubin, France, 15, 22
St. Nazaire, France, 4, 7
Stalag VIIIB (prison camp), 38–41
Stalin, Premier Joseph, 5, *5*, 14
Thrussel, Les, 46
Tirpitz (German battleship), 7

V-W-Y
Vaagso, Norway, 4, 7
Vaillancourt, Corporal Donatien, 45, *45*
Valois, Sister Agnès Marie, 37, *37*, 45, *45*
Varengeville, 15
Victoria Cross, 19, 33, 34, 46
Warren, Bruce, 29, *29*, 46
Warren, Douglas, 29, *29*, 46
Whitaker, Captain Denis, 9, *9*, 13, 26, 46
White Beach, 15, 26
Yellow Beach, 15, 17, 18
Young, Major Peter, 17, 18–19, *19*

Selected Bibliography

Atkin, Ronald. *Dieppe 1942: The Jubilee Disaster.* London: Macmillan, 1980.

Berton, Pierre. *Marching As To War.* Toronto: Random House, 2001.

Chéron, Philippe, Thierry Chion, and Olivier Richard. *Dieppe: Operation Jubilee.* Darnetal Cedex: Petit à Petit, 2002.

Christie, N.M. *The Suicide Raid: The Canadians at Dieppe.* Ottawa: CEF Books, 2000.

Granatstein, J.L. *The Last Good War.* Vancouver: Douglas & McIntyre, 2005.

Greenhous, Brereton. *Dieppe, Dieppe.* Ottawa: Editions Art Global, 1992.

Hunter, T. Murray. *Canada at Dieppe.* Ottawa: Canadian War Museum, 1982.

Leasor, James. *Green Beach.* London: William Heinemann Ltd., 1975.

Mellor, John. *Forgotten Heroes: The Canadians at Dieppe.* Toronto: Methuen, 1975.

Neillands, Robin. *The Dieppe Raid.* London: Aurum Press, 2005.

Poolton, Jack A., and Jayne Poolton-Turvey. *Destined to Survive: A Dieppe Veteran's Story.* Toronto: Dundurn Press, 1998.

Prouse, A. Robert. *Ticket to Hell Via Dieppe.* Toronto: Van Nostrand Reinhold, 1982.

Souster, Raymond. *Jubilee of Death: The Raid on Dieppe.* Ottawa: Oberon Press, 1984.

Villa, Brian Loring. *Unauthorized Action: Mountbatten and the Dieppe Raid.* Toronto: Oxford University Press, 1989.

Whitaker, Denis and Shelagh Whitaker. *Dieppe: Tragedy to Triumph.* Toronto: McGraw-Hill Ryerson, 1992.

Whitehead, William and Terence Macartney-Filgate. *Dieppe 1942: Echoes of Disaster.* Toronto: Personal Library, 1979.

Websites

The Juno Beach Centre, Veterans Affairs Canada, the CBC and **The Canadian War Museum** all have websites with useful information about Dieppe.

Picture Credits

Maps and diagrams are by Gord Sibley. Colour photographs are by Ian Brewster unless otherwise indicated.

CWM – Canadian War Museum
IWM – Imperial War Museum
LAC – Library and Archives Canada
RHLI – Royal Hamilton Light Infantry Heritage Museum
TMF – Terence Macartney-Filgate Collection

Front Cover: (Photograph) IWM/ H17477
　(Poster) LAC/C103529
　(Badge) Courtesy of Ron Reynolds
Back Cover: (Photograph) LAC/C014160
　(Nazi Poster) Private Collection
　(Badge) Courtesy of Jayne Poolton-Turvey

Endpapers: (hardcover only)
Dieppe beach today.

1: RHLI (also p. 46)
2: (Top left) IWM/Army training 10/10
　(Right) TMF
3: IWM/H12143
5: (Top left) LAC: LAC/C029589
　(Bottom left) IWM/HU10180
　(Right) IWM/HU3266
6: *The Withdrawal from Dunkirk* by Charles Cundall, IWM/LD 305

7: (Top left) IWM/A14354
　(Bottom left) IWM/H17649
　(Top right) IWM/N459
　(Bottom centre) IWM/N478
　(Bottom right) IWM/N481
8: IWM/B9473
9: (Left) IWM/B9473
　(Right) RHLI
10: (Top, poster and postcards) Author's collection
　(Bottom) IWM/B5337
11: (Left) IWM/IB122
12: (Top left) Badge and I.D. tag, courtesy of Jayne Poolton-Turvey
　(Bottom) LAC/PA144598
13: (Left) LAC/PA113243
　(Top right) IWM/B2276
　(Centre) IWM/H17477
　(Bottom) *Major General J.H. Roberts, DSO, MC* by Lawren Harris, CWM/Beaverbrook Collection of War Art, 6602-1651-1347-0300
14: Map courtesy of Royal Canadian Military Institute
16: LAC/PA171080
17: (Inset left) IWM/H18669
　(Inset right) LAC/PA 1113244
18: (Bottom) IWM/HU1833
　(Top left) IWM/H2256
　(Centre) IWM/H22605
　(Right) IWM/A11
19: (Inset left) Jubilee Association
　(Inset right) TMF

20: (Top) TMF
　(Bottom left) Illustration by Gordon Wilson
　(Bottom right) TMF
21: (Inset) Courtesy of Jayne Poolton-Turvey
22: (Top inset) RHLI
23: Illustration by Gordon Wilson
24: (Left) LAC/PA113245
　(Right) Illustration by Gordon Wilson
　(Badge) RHLI
25: (Top) From *Green Beach* by James Leasor
　(Bottom left) Bundesarchiv/Bild: 1011-291-1202-37
　(Bottom right) Bundesarchiv/Bild: 1011-343-0656-30
26: (Top) TMF
　(Bottom) Courtesy of Fred Engelbrecht
27: *Dieppe Raid* by Charles Fraser Comfort, 1946, Beaverbrook Collection of War Art, CWM/19710261-2183
28: TMF
29: (Top left) LAC/PA183772
　(Bottom left) IWM/A11242
　(Top right) Shutterstock
　(Inset, flyers) Courtesy of Duke Warren
　(Dornier) Bundesarchiv/Bild: 1011-341-0489-10A
　(Bottom right) RHLI
30: (Top left) LAC/BH14839
　(Top right) LAC/PA113247
　(Bottom) LAC/PA183770
31: (Top) LAC/C014160
　(Bottom, poster) LAC/C103528
32: (Top left) LAC/C029861
　(Top centre) IWM/A11240
　(Top right) IWM/A11238
　(Bottom) TMF

33: LAC/183773
　(Poster) Canadian War Poster Collection, Rare Books and Special Collections, McGill University Library, WP2.V1.F1
34: (Top left) LAC/C014171
　(Top right) TMF
　(Bottom) Illustration by Sharif Tarabay
35: (Top) TMF
　(Right) *Casualty on the Beach at Dieppe* by Alfred Hierl, 1945, Beaverbrook Collection of War Art CWM/19710261-5976
　(Bottom) RHLI
36: TMF
37: (Top left) TMF
　(Right) Jubilee Association
　(Inset, wedding) TMF
38: (Top and centre) RHLI
　(Bottom) TMF
39: (Top, centre and bottom right) Royal Regiment Museum
　(Bottom left) Juno Beach Centre
40: (Left) TMF
　(Right top) Courtesy of Jayne Poolton-Turvey
　(Right bottom) From *Ticket to Hell* by A. Robert Prouse
41: (Left and right) TMF
42: (Top left) IWM/BU3865
　(Centre) Courtesy of Jayne Poolton-Turvey
　(Bottom) Ron Reynolds
43: (Top left) Bundesarchiv/Bild 146-1971-052-27
　(Top centre) IWM/B10480
　(Top right) LAC/PA131233
　(Bottom) LAC/PA176696
48: RHLI

Produced by Whitfield Editions
Designed by Gordon Sibley

Library and Archives Canada Cataloguing in Publication

Brewster, Hugh
Dieppe: Canada's darkest day of World War II / Hugh Brewster.

ISBN 978-0-545-99420-0 (bound).
ISBN 978-0-545-99421-7 (pbk.)

1. Dieppe Raid, 1942 — Juvenile literature.
2. Canada — Armed Forces — History — World War, 1939-1945 — Juvenile literature.
3. World War, 1939-1945 — Canada— Juvenile literature. I. Title.

D756.5.D5B72 2008　　j940.54'21425
C2008-903107-5

ISBN 10 0-545-99420-9

SCHOLASTIC CANADA LTD.
604 King Street West
Toronto, Ontario, Canada
M5V 1E1

4 3 2 Printed in Singapore 46 09 10 11
First printing June 2009

About the Author Hugh Brewster won the Children's Literature Roundtables of Canada Information Book Award for *On Juno Beach* in 2005. *At Vimy Ridge* was the Honour Book for the same award in 2007 and won the Norma Fleck Award for Non-Fiction in 2008. He is the author of a number of other award-winning books for young readers, including: *Anastasia's Album; Inside the Titanic; The Other Mozart; Carnation, Lily, Lily, Rose;* and *Breakout Dinosaurs.* For more information go to: www.hughbrewster.com.

Acknowledgments Particular thanks go to Dieppe veterans and their families for sharing memories and mementoes: Jayne Poolton-Turvey, daughter of Jack Poolton; Fred Engelbrecht and Lynda Hook; Ron Reynolds and his wife, Margaret. In Dieppe, thanks are due to Marcel Diologent of the Jubilee Association, Olivier Richard, and Peter and Madeleine Mitchell. Particular thanks go to Terence Macartney-Filgate for access to his extensive photograph collection and useful book about Dieppe. I'm grateful to the museums and their helpful staff who allowed us to photograph their artifacts: Marie-Josée Lafond at the Juno Beach Centre; Captain Bruce Barbeau at the Royal Regiment Museum; Stan Overy of the Royal Hamilton Light Infantry Heritage Museum and Gregory Loughton of the Royal Canadian Military Institute. Thanks go to Gordon Wilson for his accurate illustrations of Dieppe battle scenes and to Sharif Tarabay; to my nephew and travelling companion, Ian Brewster, for his colour photographs; to Gord Sibley for his excellent design; and to my long-time colleague and editor, Sandra Bogart Johnston. Special thanks to Terry Copp of the Laurier Centre for Military, Strategic and Disarmament Studies for his expert review and comments.